THE STORY OF
David
Livingstone

KT-430-406

CORBIE

SHUTTLE ROW

Imagine this is you – nine years old, in Scotland, less than two hundred years ago. You get up at half past five in the morning. The house is cold and dark – no heating, no electric light. Your breakfast is cold oatmeal that has been soaking in sour milk and water. Then it's off to work. By six, you must be at the Mill. It's not far – just along the road, belching out coal smoke from its high chimney.

All day you will be there, working at your machine. You are a Piecer, working with two other children on the spinning frame. Your job is to watch the strands of cotton as the machine spins them into cloth, and bring them together if they become too tight, or snap. You have to watch closely, all the time. Sometimes you have to crawl over or under the machine while it is still working. There will be a short break when you can sit with the other workers and have your lunch piece – a bit of bannock and cheese, with water to drink. Then it's back to work. The rest of the day drags on. It is hot and damp in the factory. You begin to get tired, but you mustn't stop checking the threads. The spinner will shout at you if you do. The foreman will be walking up and down the factory floor. If he thinks you are not paying attention, he gives you a whack with his stick.

If you are sleepy, he will get someone to throw a bucketful of cold water over you. It is now evening but you go on working. When at last you stop it is eight o' clock at night.

This is what it is like for the young David Livingstone from Monday to Saturday every week. Only on a Sunday do the machines stop. His pay for all this work is very small – child workers are cheap. It doesn't take him long to count his pay. There have been no school days for David. He has been taught at home by his father to read and to count.

Surely the Mill is enough work for anyone to do? Most of the other children think so. They are so tired when they go home that there is no playing or singing.

But David is different. He is just as tired as they are but he hasn't finished working. From eight o'clock to ten o'clock at night, he now goes to the company school, along with a few others, mostly older than him. While they are learning to read, he is learning Latin from a book. Even during the short midday break at the Mill, when the other children sit around talking, he sits by himself with his head in his book.

"Come on," they shout. "Put that book away. What do you think you are? Mill-boys don't need book-learning."

"What do you think you are?" David doesn't know the answer to that question. He knows who he is – his name is David Livingstone. He knows where he lives –

in Shuttle Row, in Blantyre. His father sells tea from door to door and hands out Bible leaflets at the same time. His mother keeps the one-room home, where the whole family lives, as neat and clean as she can in a place where there is no running water.

On Sunday, David goes to church with his parents and his brothers and sisters – it is a big family. Only then, after church, can he go out. Once he got a Sunday job from a farmer who paid him a penny to watch over his cows. But one day he found David reading a book while the cows strayed out of the gate. That was the end of that.

Why is David doing all this extra learning? There is something inside him that makes him want to – however tired he is. He is keen to learn as much as he can about the world. He wants to please two people – one he sees every day – his father, Neil Livingstone. The other he cannot see but he always feels he is there and that is God. Nothing else frightens him but he is rather frightened by the idea of God, up there, beyond the sky, watching him. Sometimes he wonders what God wants David Livingstone to do. Will he get it right?

THE DOCTOR

Ten years go by. Nothing changes in David's world, except that he grows bigger – no longer a boy but a young man. At the age of nineteen, he becomes a Spinner at the Mill. Three young Piecers now mind the threads on his frame.

But some things have changed inside David. Now he knows what he wants to do, and it is not to stay at the Mill in Blantyre. He has come to believe something he did not know when he was a boy of ten – God is love. Now, he wants to tell other people about God's love.

The way to do this is to become both a doctor and a missionary. He will then go out to Africa. Most people at this time know very little about this huge continent. As a doctor, he will help the African people to get well from all the illnesses they suffer from. As a missionary, he will teach them the story of the Bible.

It means more hard work. He has to go back to the Mill in summer-time to earn the money he needs to go to college. At Anderson's University in Glasgow, he begins to learn how to be a doctor. Then he says goodbye to his family for a while and goes to Ongar, outside London, where he learns his other business – how to be a missionary for the Christian Church. Back in Scotland again, he finally qualifies as a doctor. For the Mill-boy from Shuttle Row, it is a great achievement. But he is David Livingstone and his achievements have only just begun.

THE MISSIONARY

At last, in December 1840, Dr David Livingstone, now a man of 27, leaves London on the sailing ship *George*, bound for South Africa. From the very start, he loves Africa. And he also finds that he loves travelling despite the fact that travel through Africa is very difficult at this time, with no roads, no towns and nowhere to stay. Big lumbering covered wagons pulled by oxen make slow progress. It takes nearly two months to reach his destination, the mission station at Kuruman. There, David tries to settle down to the life of a missionary, but he has his own ideas about what he should be doing. He believes that God has brought him to Africa and that there is some great task in front of him.

After three years, the London Missionary Society, his employers, allow him to open a mission station of his own, far from any other, in the valley of Mabotsa. Missionaries have no one to help them. They must build their own houses, plant their own crops, look after themselves in every way. Before they can teach the Gospel, they have to learn the African languages.

We have seen that David is very strong-willed and determined, even as a young boy. He is also very lucky. Mabotsa is plagued by wild roaming lions. Called by the villagers when a lion attacks their sheep, David

shoots at it but only wounds it. The angry lion jumps at him, catches him by the shoulder and shakes him, as he says later, "like a terrier dog shakes a rat." One of David's native helpers, Mebalwe, fires another gun and the lion drops David to attack him and another man, before falling dead from David's shot. All the men are seriously wounded but fortunate to be alive. David's arm is slashed and splintered; he must heal himself as well as his friends. He will never again be able to lift his left arm higher than his shoulder. A good thing he is right-handed!

Soon after this he finds himself a wife – Mary Moffat, the daughter of Robert Moffat, the founder of the mission station at Kuruman. Like David, she is Scottish, but Mary has lived in Africa since she was four. From Mabotsa they move to Chonuane, to set up another new station – David Livingstone is always happiest when, as he wrote, he "lives beyond other men's line of things." He finds it hard to get on with the other missionaries but easy to talk to the Africans. Unlike many other Europeans, he tries hard to understand their way of life and to respect their customs.

David and Mary lead a very hard life. There is no rain, and no crops grow. Some of the Africans blame David for keeping the rain away. From Chonuane they move to Kolobeng when the African chief moves his tribe there. For a year they live in a tiny hut, burningly hot in summer and freezingly cold in winter. In five years,

Mary has five children. One of them dies, as a tiny baby. The others, two boys and two girls, survive. In a letter to a friend, David writes, "Crowds of flies continually settled on the eyes of our poor little brats by day." The children get used to some strange food. When there is nothing else, they sometimes eat locusts and wild honey, like John the Baptist in the Bible. They also eat caterpillars and frogs. In fact, in most ways they lead the same lives as the little African children of the Bakwain tribe, except that every morning and night, they have to say their prayers. But often they cry with hunger.

The African chief, Sechele, one day agrees to become a Christian. David is delighted and hopes that this will lead to the rest of the Bakwain tribe becoming converted. Sadly, he soon has to report that Sechele has gone back to his old ways.

The river at Kolobeng dries up. The plants and even the trees are dying. David Livingstone is forced to think about what he is doing. Is this to be his great achievement? He is still determined to bring the news of Jesus to the African tribes, but now he sees that there is another way. Nobody has explored into the heart of the great African continent. Ever since he came to Africa, David has wanted to do this. He has heard stories of mighty rivers, lakes, and waterfalls. This will be his mission – to open up Africa, not by building roads, but by following the great rivers.

THE EXPLORER

David begins his explorations while still at Kolobeng. On one journey, he takes Mary and their three young children Robert, Agnes and Thomas, across the Kalahari Desert and back again, in boiling heat. Once they went without water for two days. It was after this that Mary had the baby who died. Despite this, David takes them on another long journey across the same terrible desert, and the children nearly die from lack of water. "The less there was of water, the more thirsty the little rogues became," writes David, in a grim sort of joke. He himself is ready to bear any hardship, and he thinks his children should be as hardy and bold as he is. At the end of this awful wilderness journey, he finds a vast river, the Zambesi. Although it is more than a thousand miles from the sea, it is five hundred yards wide. Perhaps this is the great way into unknown Africa?

At this time David realises that his new life of exploration and travel is not suitable for a young family. It is decided that Mary and the children will go to Scotland, a faraway country that she does not remember and they have never seen. A long journey to Cape Town follows, and David waves goodbye as they set off on the steamship.

Now he is on his own, and he can follow up his plan.

He makes a long and difficult journey, partly through flooded swamps, to meet another African tribe, the Makololo. He hopes that he will find there a good place to start a new settlement, where traders will come and deal fairly with the Africans, and which can also be a centre for other missionaries to work in. He also keeps on looking for his great dream – a river on which ships can sail from the sea right into the heart of Africa.

On his search, David's African guides lead him to

Mosi-da-Tunya, "The Smoke That Thunders" – a huge waterfall, more than one and a half kilometres wide and 120 metres high, where the Zambesi pours over a cliff and flows on through a mighty gorge. He names it Victoria Falls, after the Queen. But he is not overjoyed by such a magnificent sight. He would rather there was no waterfall, for no ship can get past there. But perhaps ships will be able to come up close to it – he has not yet explored down the great river. Whilst looking for rivers suitable for ships, David becomes the first man from Europe to walk right across Africa, from the Atlantic Ocean to the Indian Ocean. Often ill, suffering from hunger, thirst, disease, poisoned cuts and scratches, he never gives up. He believes that he is doing God's work, and that God is watching over him.

There are other men doing very different work. David Livingstone is exploring Africa because he believes it will help the Africans to learn about Europe, about Christianity and about the business of trading. Others, like the Portuguese Silva Porto, are exploring Africa because they want to take away African people as slaves. David is horrified to find that his friends, the Makololo, are helping to catch and sell men, women and children from other tribes. Everywhere David goes, he finds that the slave traders have been there before him. Many Africans think David is a slave trader himself. Some of the slave traders pretend they are David's friends, in order to win the Africans' trust.

Then, using their guns to frighten their victims, they choose the strongest-looking ones and march them away, with their necks caught in forked sticks and their hands tied. Many fall ill on the way and are killed by the pitiless traders. Those who survive will be sold like cattle, forced to work for no pay and kept like prisoners.

By this time, the inhuman practice of slavery has been abolished in Britain but many other countries still use slaves, and this snatching and selling of human beings is another reason why David wants to open up ways into Africa. More and more, David realises that the slave trade has got to be stopped before the real work of the missionaries can begin.

At the end of more than three thousand miles of walking through trackless jungle and rough rocky trails, David returns to Britain again, his first visit home for sixteen years. He finds that he is now a famous man. His reports of his travels and discoveries have reached home before him. Soon he will be well off for the first time in his life, when his book, *Missionary Travels*, becomes a best-seller.

Everyone wants to meet Dr Livingstone, shake his hand, hear him speak. He is called to meet Queen Victoria. A great deal of money is collected to help the missionaries in Africa. For David, the boy from the Blantyre mills, it is a strange experience. He is glad to be with his family again – but he is so busy meeting people, giving talks and writing a book about his travels that he does not have much time to spend with his children. But Mary will be coming with him on the next expedition. For David is returning to the River Zambesi, this time to sail up from its mouth into the heart of Africa, in a ship, the *Pearl*. To get as far up the river as possible, the *Pearl* is carrying the parts of another, smaller ship, the *Ma-Robert*. This was the African's name for Mary, meaning Robert's Mother (Robert had been their first child, back in Kolobeng). But Mary finds she is expecting another baby and has to stay behind in South Africa when the *Pearl* sails on.

The *Ma-Robert* is not much of a ship; David describes her engine as being more like a coffee grinder. Her hull is soon full of leaks. But much worse, David finds that the Zambesi is useless as a river highway. Sandbanks, shallows, rapids and waterfalls make it impossible to steam up-river. Turning up a side-stream instead, he

finds the way to a great lake, which he calls Lake Nyasa (now Lake Malawi, and the second-largest lake in Africa). Here, too, he finds the slave traders have arrived before him. David wants to have a new ship sent, in parts, to be assembled on the shore of the lake and prevent slave traders sailing across. When the government refuses to pay for it, he does so himself, out of his own money.

This ship, the *Lady Nyasa*, never reaches the lake. David's expedition is costing the government too much money, and has to come to an end. These four years are the worst in David's life. At the end of the expedition, Mary comes back again to join him, but after only three months together, she dies of fever. David has the sad task of writing to tell his children that they will never see their mother again.

What can be done with the *Lady Nyasa*? Nobody wants her. Undaunted, David navigates his little ship across the stormy Indian Ocean to Bombay, to sell it in that busy harbour. From there he returns to Britain. He is still famous but the failure of the Zambesi Expedition means he is not such a hero as on his first return. David is not worried. He still believes God has a task for him, and he intends to go back to Africa and finish it.

At this time, there is great interest in finding where the Nile, the longest river in Africa, starts from. Surely David is the man for this. He takes on the job, but not, as he says, just to fill in a blank space on the map of the world. He wants to put an end to the slave trade, and he believes that if he finds the source of the Nile, he will be so famous that he will be able to stop this great wickedness. And so David sets out for Africa for the last time.

JOURNEY'S END

As we know, David Livingstone has wanted all his life to go beyond what other men have done. In the last years of his life, he goes far beyond where any man from Europe has been before. Often ill, often hungry, he is determined not to go back to Britain until he has found the source of the Nile. He is certain that this will be an important step towards his great aim, to set Africa free from the evils of the slave trade.

The years pass by. From where David is, in the heart of Africa, there is no chance of sending letters back to Scotland. Many people believe that he is dead. After five years, sick and exhausted, hoping to find letters and supplies of food and medicine, he makes his slow way back to the Arab trading post of Ujiji. But almost all the supplies have been stolen, and any letters lost or thrown away. Then one day, he hears astounding news. Another white man is on the way. This is an English journalist, Henry Morton Stanley, who has been sent by an American newspaper to find Dr Livingstone. As he comes up to David, sitting in front of a wattle hut, Stanley says four words that will become famous:

"Dr Livingstone, I presume?"

Stanley stays with David for several months, and though he begs David to go back with him, David refuses. His work is not finished. Stanley returns alone, to report to the world that David Livingstone's great quest continues. David returns to his explorations. Stanley has arranged to send up new porters and fresh supplies from the coast, and with these, David heads back into the jungles and marshes. But he is a very sick man, too ill to travel as he used to. Susi, one of his faithful African helpers, carries David on his back across the rivers, and in the end he has to be carried on a sort of stretcher. In a tiny African village, the journey finally comes to an end. David Livingstone, after more than thirty years of gruelling struggle, dies. In his last moments, he crawls from his bed to the floor and kneeling, he prays to God, whose work he has done for so long.

So David Livingstone did not live to find the source of the Nile or to see the end of the slave trade. But, as we have seen, he had achieved many other things. His life and ideals inspired many thousands of other people. And today, he is remembered not only in Scotland, where he was born, and in England, where his body lies buried in Westminster Abbey, but also in Africa as one who was a lover of that great continent and a true friend to its peoples.